Understanding the Challenge of "NO" for Children with Autism

Improving Communication
Increasing Positivity
Enhancing Relationships

Colette McNeil

For information, contact
MSI Press
1760-F Airline Highway, #203
Hollister, CA 95023

Cover designed by Carl Leaver

Library of Congress Control Number 2017957366

ISBN: 978-1-942891-76-5

Contents

Colette McNeil

Acknowledgements

I would like to thank, first and foremost, the hundreds of amazing children who shared themselves so authentically with me over my 20 years of teaching. These children with autism and other disabilities taught me more than I could ever teach them. I thank the children's families for sharing their loved ones and themselves so courageously. And finally, I am appreciative of my coworkers with whom my journey was shared and who influenced my perspectives along the way.

I am ever grateful for the continued learning and loving experience of having a close personal relationship with my nephew with autism and his family, who I hold dear to my heart.

For his support in the production of this book, I would like to thank my brother/roommate/friend for listening to my ideas, encouraging me in my endeavors, reading many attempted drafts and courageously sharing his candid impressions to support improved versions of each segment. I thank my parents for their undying support, encouragement and suggestions as my writing progressed over time. And a special thank-you goes out to my friend who graciously offered to read and provide editorial suggestions

Colette McNeil

for the manuscript. You are all so kind and giving. I am blessed to have each of you in my life.

Preface

AUTISM SPECTRUM DISORDERS

Diagnostic and Statistical Manual of Mental Disorders, (Fifth Edition) **(2013). American Psychiatric Association (p. 31-32).**
(DSM-5)

Autism Spectrum disorder is characterized by persistent deficits in social communication and social interaction across multiple contexts, including deficits in social reciprocity, nonverbal communicative behaviors used for social interaction, and skills in developing, maintaining, and understanding relationships. In addition to the social communication deficits the diagnosis of autism spectrum disorder requires the presence of restricted repetitive patterns of behavior, interests, or activities.

Colette McNeil

No

Merriam Webster Dictionary
merriam-webster.com

No – adverb \'nō\

1. **a** *chiefly Scotland*: <u>not</u>
   b —used as a function word to express the negative of an alternative choice or possibility *shall we go out to dinner or no*

2. in no respect or degree —used in comparisons you're no better than the rest of us

3. not so —used to express negation, dissent, denial, or refusal no, I'm not going

4. used with a following adjective to imply a meaning expressed by the opposite positive statement in no uncertain terms

5. used as a function word to emphasize a following negative or to introduce a more emphatic, explicit, or comprehensive statement it's big, no, it's gigantic

6. used as an interjection to express surprise, doubt, or incredulity

7. used in combination with a verb to form a compound adjective no-bake pie

8. in negation shook his head no

No – adjective

1. *a*: not any *no parking no disputing the decision*
   b: hardly any: very little *finished in no time*

2. not a: quite other than a *he's no expert*

3. used in combination with a noun to form a compound adjective *a no-nonsense realist*

No – noun

4. an act or instance of refusing or denying by the use of the word *no*: <u>denial</u> *received a firm no in reply*

5. *a*: a negative vote or decision
   b: **noes** *or* **nos** *plural*: persons voting in the negative

Pragmatics

Merriam Webster Dictionary
merriam-webster.com

Pragmatics – noun, plural in form but singular or plural in construction: \prag-'ma-tiks\

1. a branch of semiotics that deals with the relation between signs or linguistic expressions and their users

2. a branch of linguistics that is concerned with the relationship of sentences to the environment in which they occur

3. *linguistics*: the study of what words mean in particular situations

Colette McNeil

Chapter 1
Introduction

No,
A tiny little word
So often heard
So why, oh why
Does it make you cry?

I invite you on a journey in unfolding small layers of awareness, illuminating how thoughtfully chosen vocabulary can greatly enhance your relationship with a child with autism. *Understanding the Challenge of - NO - for Children with Autism: Improving Communication - Increasing Positivity - Enhancing Relationships* focuses solely on the use of this one tiny word. Yet, it illustrates the far-reaching implications that one word can have in determining the very essence of our daily interactions with children with autism.

COREY

Giggling so hard he almost loses his balance, on tippy-toes, bouncing foot to foot, arms swaying in the air, 3-year-old Corey celebrates with joy as he watches Alice approach.

"Uh Oh! Corey thinks this is a game. I probably shouldn't have been so playful."

Alice has removed Corey from the tabletop three times in the last three minutes. Each time keeping the interaction light, she spiritedly engaged, "Oh no, no, no, little man. We don't stand on tables. Get down." He was then scooped up in a hug, spun away from the table and gently placed with his feet on the floor.

Now, standing next to the table, Alice speaks in a more subdued, neutral tone, "No, get down."

Corey gleefully throws his hands up and rests his body against hers. Alice makes an effort to lower Corey down to the ground calmly, without the excitable performance of earlier exchanges. Over the next few minutes, Corey and Alice repeat this cycle several more times. Alice hopes that delivering a passive response will counteract the silliness of before and dissuade Corey from continuing his game. Unfortunately, Corey persists in his cheerful pursuit.

In an effort to alleviate the temptation to climb, Alice walks Corey away from the enticing table and sets him on a beanbag chair to look at a book. Hopeful that he is content, Alice leaves Corey to play independently.

Jumping to his feet, Corey runs across the room, scales the chair and is quickly upon the table. Standing tall on his toes, pressing his chin into his hands, Corey keeps intensely watchful eyes on Alice.

Across the room, leaning forward, hands on her hips, Alice uses a reprimanding tone, "NO Corey."

Corey stands silent in anticipation.

Alice firmly directs, "NO—Get down!"

Letting out a high-pitched squeal, Corey explodes into jubilation and prances about the table.

Stifling a chuckle, Alice stares at Corey, perplexed by the contradiction between her reprimand and Corey's unabashed exuberance. Realizing that Corey has misunderstood her words and seems unaffected by her change in tone and body language, Alice reflectively queries, what now? Making further effort to project a firm demeanor, Alice moves closer, repeating slowly, "NO—Get down."

Instantly, Corey flashes a Cheshire cat grin and beckons to be lifted.

Dismayed, Alice realizes, *Corey doesn't understand my, "No," and thinks the phrase, "Get Down," means I am going to pick him up.*

Pondering her next action, Alice gives Corey a hug but does not move him to the floor. Racking her brain for a better way to build understanding, she contemplates, *What do I want him to do when I say, "Get down?" Ideally, I want him to climb down by himself.* Pointing to the chair, Alice gently pulls his little hand downward and tells Corey to get down. Corey thrusts himself upwards and prepares to be lifted.

Well, that didn't work. Pensively, Alice watches Corey dance upon the table while continuing to ruminate on the problem. *I don't want to lift him off the table. What specifically do I want Corey to do? I do not want him to jump off or have him try to walk off by stepping on the chair. No, I want him to crawl down in a controlled manner on his own. So, how do I get him to climb down? He doesn't understand my words, body language or gestures. I am going to have to motor him through it. He will be confused and could get upset. I need to be ready to keep him from falling if he throws a tantrum.*

With her plan in place, Alice begins, "Corey, get down."

Corey reaches up but is stopped from delivering his hug.

"No." Turning Corey around, "Get down," Alice assists him to his hands and knees, aids him to lower his legs to

3

the chair, repositions his hands and continues until he is stably planted below.

Standing on the surface, Corey gives Alice a quizzical look and immediately ascends the table.

Recognizing the need to practice this new directive, Alice allows Corey to climb unimpeded. Once Corey is standing, Alice repeats, "Get down."

Corey throws his hands up and smiles broadly.

"No," Alice again turns Corey around and assists him in his descent, repeating, "Get down."

As soon as his feet hit the ground, Corey determinedly jets from Alice's grasp and quickly scrambles aloft once more.

Alice waits for Corey to be upright atop the table before delivering her instruction, "Get down."

Corey predictively extends his arms toward Alice.

"No."

When his embrace is blocked, Corey cries out in exasperation. As Alice prompts Corey to turn his body, he begins weeping and pulls away from her. Corey independently crawls down to the floor, runs to the beanbag chair and pouts.

Understanding his frustration, Alice engages Corey positively, praising him for sitting on the beanbag chair and showing him a book. Corey remains upset with Alice and turns away from her. While sitting with Corey, Alice compassionately resolves, *I must be more careful in the future. I thought I was being sweet while flirtatiously redirecting him with my gentle, "no, no, no," but what I really did was confuse him. I will work on being clearer in pairing my words and actions. It's not fair to confound Corey by being playful then expect compliance on an instruction he doesn't understand.*

Breaking it Down

Communication breakdowns regularly dissolve into expressed emotional distress on the part of both children with autism and their guardians. Parents, family members, teachers and caregivers strive to build affirmative social relationships with the children in their lives. Playfulness, kind words, gentle interactions, smiles and hugs are all positive influences in relating to children. Providing instruction, protecting for safety, and teaching behavioral competencies are also realities of loving guardianship. The effort to maintain positivity and emotional attunement while engaged in safeguarding and instructing youngsters is a ceaseless balancing act. While there is clearly profound love and attachment between the adults and children, there are also many daily challenges to maintaining positive social interactions such as in the story of Corey. Conventional wisdom may point to these negative outcomes as problems of training, instruction, discipline and speech production. I posit that common, habitual communication styles are at the crux of the issue.

In this book, I focus on the use of the word, "No," in our daily interactions. Yet, I am hopeful that the underlying concepts explored within will be found generalizable to other practices of communication and engagement when supporting children with autism.

So, what does the word, "No," have to do with enhancing your relationship with a child with autism? Well, that answer balances on an investigation into the challenges related to the child's autism, the everyday uses of, "No," and the convergence of these two topics. In the following chapters I will illustrate how, "No," is unintentionally used in ways that sabotage understanding, emotional regulation, social confidence, and relational attunement. I find a line in the movie *Experimenter* apropos to my endeavor, "Awareness is the first step to our Liberation." It is my hope that as communication roadblocks are illuminated, adults may become thoughtful in choosing vocabulary that improves communication, increases positivity, and enhances relationships.

Chapter 2
No Running

Raise your hand if you have found yourself plugging along on a multiple-choice test when you were stopped cold, or at least had to slow down and look more carefully at a question stated in the negative: "Which statement is NOT correct?" Or worse yet, a double negative: "Which answer does not disagree with the following statement?" Huh? Okay, slow down. I'm looking for the *incorrect* answer and the answer that *agrees* with the statement. Why did the instructor have to be so tricky? As my hand is elevated along with yours, I admit to having gotten more than a few of these answers wrong throughout my education. In my groove, working steadily along, I was busy looking for the correct answers, not the incorrect ones, and I didn't read the question carefully enough. As scholars, it is our responsibility to read carefully and decipher the negatives in order to respond correctly. The instructor may choose to help the learners by writing the questions more clearly but does not assume the responsibility to do so. Students must apply critical thinking skills and answer accurately if they do not want to suffer the consequences of a lower grade.

"No Running"

Lined-up in the hallway Miss Leaky's primary school class of children with autism await their liberation to morning recess. Praising their cooperation, Mr. Compos says, "Okay, let's go play." The students are full of energy and begin jogging down the hall. Mr. Compos calls out, "No running." With joyful expressions, their momentum boils up to a bounding stride. Mr. Compos repeats, "No running," but they break into a sprint, bursting out onto the blacktop.

At the play structure, Mr. Compos gathers the students together, explains that there is no running in the halls and imposes a one-minute break from playing as a consequence. The students complain about the unfairness of Mr. Compos, but are soon off to play.

Later, before heading to P.E. Miss Leaky reminds the schoolmates, "We walk in the hallway." She then instructs the line leader to guide the way to P.E. class, reminding, "Walking." The gang begins walking steadily, then quicken their steps. Miss Leaky announces, "Walking," and the friends slow again, cooperatively heading to their destination.

Returning from outside, the pupils are hungry for lunch and anxious to get their meal items. Mr. Compos reiterates, "No running in the hallway." The group walks excitedly then quickly expands into a trot. Mr. Compos broadcasts, "No running." Their pace quickens. Mr. Compos states again, more firmly, "No running!" but increasing in speed, the set narrowly miss a collision with another group. In the schoolroom, feeling frustrated, Mr. Compos recounts the rules and consequences for running down the hall. Ignoring their grievances, Mr. Compos assigns the class three minutes of quiet-time before being discharged to lunch.

Finally gathered for the transition to the cafeteria, Miss Leaky stands facing the line and provides a reminder to the children, "Walking in the hall." She leads the group, but the anxious students begin to speed past her. Mr. Compos warns, "No running," with no effect.

Miss Leaky then states, "Walking," and the students reduce the swiftness of their gait until coolly ambling to the tables.

Departing the lunchroom, the children make their way down the hall to the field for afternoon recess. Reminders of expectations and consequences are delivered. The youngsters start out obligingly. As their excitement bubbles up, they once again hasten their steps. Mr. Compos cautions, "No running," yet the speed remains accelerated.

When Miss Leaky states, "Walking," the children slow their pace somewhat.

Miss Leaky reminds, "Nice walking."

The group's excitement quells and remains contained through the final length of the corridor. As soon as their feet meet the grass, Miss Leaky's release, "Okay, running," is answered by wild bursts of motion as students dart across the field.

Prior to leaving recess, the class lines-up once again, and Miss Leaky reemphasizes, "Walking." The students begin traveling moderately, but quickly cultivate hurriedness. Mr. Compos' warning, "No running," proves ineffective. Copying Miss Leaky, Mr. Compos exclaims, "Walking," and the students instantly reduce their momentum.

Miss Leaky compliments the students, "Good walking," which inspires a relaxed stroll approaching the classroom. Pleased, Mr. Compos gives everyone a high-five as they enter the room.

Breaking it Down

Communication

No running, No jumping, No talking, No shoes – No shirt – No service. Speaking in this style of negative phrasing is as common and ingrained as answering the telephone with, "Hello." To the majority of society, the message is direct, concise, and typically easily understood. Unfortunately, children with autism struggle with deciphering statements requesting the negation of an action. While it is not impossible for these children to learn some regularly used negative statements, it takes more effort and exposure to the exact phrasing to produce understanding.

If we look carefully at the information provided by current researchers and practitioners of autism we could pinpoint some of the children's receptive communication difficulties. Autism causes deficits, to varying degrees, in the ability to understand verbal sounds and attach meaning to them. Further, if the children do understand the individual spoken words, they may not be able to fully process strings of auditory information or words in sentences. Many children with autism will often be able to comprehend and respond to either the first word, or more likely the last word, of a sentence. It is my experience that children with autism most often respond to the very last thing they hear.

In the story above, Mr. Compos is calling out to the students, "No running," and the students are only processing, "Running." Therefore, they gleefully continue onward. For the children, this situation is not unlike test takers answering questions written in the double negative form. Mr. Compos is requesting the negation of running and expecting the students to decipher this negation and translate it into the correct response.

When speaking in a negation of action style, we are asking the recipient not only to process the sounds into meaningful concepts but also to employ critical thinking skills to decipher an indirect message. Further, if the children do understand the statement, "No running," to mean cease the action, there is no information given that indicates what other action is expected. What is the request, "No running," asking the student to do; skip, gallop, walk, tiptoe, crawl, stop? While the message may seem clear to the speaker, the receiving child with autism is often oblivious to the full implication of the statement. In this example, the students hold the responsibility for understanding the complicated message and are provided a consequence for getting it wrong. Mr. Compos repeatedly gives the students time-out for responding incorrectly to his instruction.

*Tell the students what **to do** versus what **not to do**.*

Barbara Bloomfield

Miss Leaky's approach provides the students a clear message of what *to do* instead of what *not to do*. Miss Leaky accepts the responsibility for choosing her vocabulary carefully to communicate at the comprehension level of the students. Miss Leaky's statement, "Walking," provided the class the exact action being requested and did so using only one clearly spoken word.

Supplementary Influences

It turns out that our brains are literally hardwired to perform at their best not when they are negative or even neutral, but when they are positive.

Shawn Achor

Colette McNeil

"Smile when you answer the phone," is a piece of advice commonly found in training protocols for receptionists. The principle behind this advice is that smiling changes the position of the structures in the mouth in a manner that raises the tone of voice to a higher pitch. This higher pitch sounds pleasant and welcoming. In our story, as a side effect of using the single words expressing what to do, especially when using the form of present participle, "Walking," Miss Leaky sounds more pleasant and less demanding. This change in tone inspires a pleasing affect that is received well by the students and by observers in the environment. In her book Presence, Amy Cuddy explains the findings of her research on how one's body posture can have positive or negative effects on one's mood. She shares that closed postures, such as arms folded across the body and head down, result in a more negative mood whereas open postures, such as arms out to the sides and head tipped upward, result in positive mood. Expanding upon this concept, I propose that the use of the word, "No," when requesting the negation of actions can have a similar effect. The word, "No," tends to create a closed facial posture. The lips are pursed in a closed, rounded position, the cheeks are draw in and forward and often the eyebrows are tipped inward and down towards the nose. I have noticed that the more my staff and I said, "No," the more frustrated we became and the harsher our tone of voice sounded. Yet when we began using the positive what to do statements, our moods were more elevated. This may be due to the better response of the students, but it seems that the raising of the voice tone when saying the, "ing," part of a request, like "Walking," which ends in a smile, not only makes us sound more pleasant, but following Amy Cuddy's line of thought, actually makes us feel more agreeable. These positive feelings result in added patience and foster amiable interactions with the children.

Relationship Dynamics

When Mr. Compos was communicating in the universally common manner, "No running," there was a domino effect of dissatisfaction and disconnection between the opposing parties. After the lack of response to his first request not to run, Mr. Compos may believe he is not being heard, and maintaining a neutral emotional state, attempt a repetition of his request. When, after the second request, the students respond opposite to Mr. Compos' expectations, he becomes frustrated with what he perceives as the students' willful disregard of his instruction. This changes his emotional state to a negative inclination. Mr. Compos then provides a consequence to the students for disobeying the rules and his commands.

In response to Mr. Compos' penalties, the students become upset by what they perceive as unfair punishment. In their perception, not only did they follow his instructions as they heard them, "Running," but they did so by increasing their efforts each time and speeding up with each repeated instruction. The students find Mr. Campos' behavior inconsistent, by first telling them to run then giving them a time-out for doing so. This perception develops confusion, negative feelings and distrust of Mr. Compos. Distrust weakens the confidence of the children, and they begin to feel uncertain and anxious around Mr. Compos. The relationship lacks attunement and all parties suffer negative emotional effects.

Miss Leaky's communication style provides meaning and inspires improvements in the children's behavior. Her single word, "Walking," tells the students what action is expected and requires the processing of only one commonly used word. The students and Miss Leaky feel confident in their interactions, as the communication between them has been perfectly aligned. Positive emotional reciprocity and attunement is achieved, and a strong relationship is reinforced.

When Mr. Compos realizes that Miss Leaky is having more success at influencing the student's actions by using the positive statement, "Walking," Mr. Compos adjusts his verbiage and is pleasantly rewarded with compliance from the students. As Mr. Compos chooses to use vocabulary that is supportive of the needs of the children, the children become amenable in their obedience. They remain in a positive emotional state, feel confident in their response to his request, and remain in tune with Mr. Campos' expectations. Consequentially, Mr. Compos obtains a positive emotional reward from communicating effectively which engenders a feeling of competence in his ability to supervise the students. Mr. Compos likewise enters a positive emotional state and shares this positivity back with the students through his social reward of a high-five. Mr. Compos and the students experience a reciprocally reinforcing moment. If Mr. Compos continues to practice shifting his vocabulary style, his relationship with the students will improve immeasurably.

I know of no more encouraging fact
than the unquestionable ability of man
to elevate his life by conscious endeavor.

Henry David Thoreau

Chapter 3
When No Means Yes

Augustus

***One Summer Day in a Class for Elementary School
Students with Autism
Story originally printed in Autism Parenting
Magazine, June, 2017***

"Good work, Josiah. You are all done! Let's check your schedule." Josiah smiles brightly and hurries to his schedule, knowing swimming is next.

As he and Miss Leaky walk through the quietly bustling classroom, a small voice calls out, "Miss Leaky, swimming?"

"Yes, Augustus, first work then swimming. Hurry up and finish your work."

Augustus smiles and continues working. Miss Leaky and Josiah walk outside and across the courtyard to the restroom.

Returning, the pair is met with a commotion of loud crying, pounding noises, and the sight of Augustus lying on his back kicking his feet.

Miss Leaky inquires, "What happened?"

Miss Ellie shares, "Augustus is mad because he was not allowed to go with Miss Alan to get ready for swimming."

Anxiously, Augustus cries out, "Miss Leaky, swimming?"

"Yes, Augustus, first work, then swimming."

Augustus shoots to his feet and returns to his tasks, only two more easy folders to go.

"Miss Ellie, swimming?" Augustus solicits.

"Finish your work, then swimming," replies Miss Ellie.

Augustus grins and increasing his pace, rushes to finish. Seeing Jean and Miss Alan walk through the door, Augustus implores, "Miss Alan, swimming?"

"No Augustus, no swimming until you finish your work!"

Instantly, the room is filled with an ear-piercing shriek, a chaotic flurry of materials flying through the air and Augustus drops to the floor, wailing. Miss Leaky approaches. Augustus pauses his frenzy, pleading, "Miss Leaky, swimming?"

"Yes Augustus, first work, then swimming," answers Miss Leaky.

Augustus weepily gathers his materials and steels himself to begin working. Tentatively, he questions, "Miss Leaky, swimming?"

Miss Leaky reassures, "Yes Augustus, good working. First work, then swimming."

Appeased, Augustus begins to complete his last few items when Miss Alan again returns from the restroom with students ready for the pool.

Augustus apprehensively voices his persistent question, "Miss Alan, swimming?"

"No Augustus, no swimming. You can't swim until you do your work!"

With rapid-fire motions papers are flung, the tipped desk slams to the floor and Augustus is again flat on his back, kicking and screaming.

Miss Leaky stands nearby and Augustus screams, "SWIMMING! MISS LEAKY, SWIMMING!"

Miss Leaky waits for that moment of silence that occurs as Augustus takes a breath, then clearly delivers a simple, "YES!"

Augustus curiously ceases his howling. Breathing heavily, he looks hesitantly at Miss Leaky then tearfully, frightfully probes, "Swimming?"

Miss Leaky's answer is slow and deliberate, "Yes Augustus, first work, then swimming."

Miss Leaky assists Augustus in reorganizing his materials, and remaining close, encourages him to finish his last folder.

Once again, Augustus anxiously asks, "Miss Alan, swimming?"

"No."

Augustus flinches.

Miss Leaky interjects, "YES SWIMMING!"

Stunned with conflicted emotion, Augustus stands wide eyed, pupils darting between Miss Alan and Miss Leaky.

Locking his gaze with hers, Miss Leaky thoughtfully enunciates her consistent retort, "YES, SWIMMING, first work, then swimming."

Miss Leaky assists Augustus to place the last two items in his folder and enthusiastically declares, "Finished! Time for swimming!"

Augustus hurries to join his classmates walking to the pool, smiles broadly, and exclaims, "SWIMMING!"

Colette McNeil

Breaking it Down

Communication

In countless social conversations, when responding to questions and requests from children such as Augustus', "May I go swimming?" many adults would start their answer with a gentle, "No," then add, "Not right now. You will go after you are done working." For a typically developing child with competent social skills and communication abilities, this is a perfectly nice answer. The child comprehends the message, *I may go swimming after I finish my task.* This understanding will inspire the child to focus and quickly complete the assignment.

For many children, the communication difficulties caused by autism block their ability to understand the full content of a message of such length and complexity. Children with autism are often only able to process the first and/or last words in lengthy verbalizations. Further, structuring the information to identify what is *not* going to happen requires an interpretation of this information into its reciprocal of what *is* going happen. The lack of any further information leaves the child to make a guess as to the correct meaning and expected response. This translation process delivers many potential inaccurate outcomes.

In the story of Augustus, our protagonist struggles in processing the entire indirect message stated in the negative, "No Augustus, no swimming. You can't swim until you do your work!" Many mainstream practitioners and trainers in autism teach that, with training, the use of short phrases and repetitive scripted sentences can build meaning for students with autism. The specifically taught short phrases are learned as language chunks that the child can process as if they were single, multisyllabic words. "I want," "Sit down," and, "Check your schedule," are examples of short phrases that children in autism-focused classrooms become adept at understanding fluidly. Phrases such as, "First—, then—," and, "Do this," become predictable cues for the children, helping them to identify that they are expected to mentally attend to the following information.

Augustus was doing fine as long as Miss Leaky used regularly scripted language and few words, stating, "Yes, first work, then swimming." He also managed well with Miss Ellie's response, which was less scripted but was still stated in a positive phrase and followed the same progression, "Finish your work, then swimming." When Miss Alan approached the question answering in a mainstream manner, "No Augustus, no swimming until you finish your work," a communication gap occurred. In this diction, Augustus likely only heard and understood the words, "No," and, "Work." He then became upset and expressed negative behaviors because he understood the message to say, "No, you will not go to the pool. You will stay in class and do work." The intent of the message is really, "*Yes, after work.*" Stating the answer in a "Yes, first/then" format, as Miss Leaky does, provides Augustus the support he needs. This statement is a direct answer that uses predictable scripted phrasing, few words, and does not need to be interpreted from the negative statement to a positive connotation.

Numerous autism researchers and practitioners hail the importance of using visual supports with students such as schedules, task lists, first/then cards, picture based expressive communication, and more. Miss Leaky's message, "Yes, first work, then swimming," is clear, concise, familiar to Augustus, and can be reinforced easily with visual supports. A visual support may be as simple as a gesture towards one item and then another while speaking. Miss Leaky could have been gesturing to Augustus' work materials and swimsuit while stating, "First work, then swimming." Other visual supports that assist communication are more concrete such as representative objects, pictures or written words. The benefit of using objects, pictures and written words is that they are constant. Spoken words are fleeting and are gone as soon as they are emitted. In the story, Miss Leaky could show Augustus pictures of work and the pool while providing her answer. Augustus could visually attend to these pictures for reassurance that he understood the answer to his question. Further, he could independently reference these pictures to remind himself that he will go swimming when he finishes his work.

Supplementary Influences

All habits are the result of our previous conditioning—things we learned to do, and then practiced them until they became what seem like a natural way to behave.

Dr. Shad Helmstetter

Over the years Augustus has ingrained behaviors to convey his negative emotional state. He has developed a habit of expressing an adverse reaction that instantly fills him with fight or flight anxiety in response to the word, "No." Relationship researcher John Gottman's findings explain that when people are feeling strong negative emotions, fight or flight responses hijack the physiology of a person and flood them with hormones, visceral reactions and emotions that overwhelm their ability to accurately receive, process and interpret information. Therefore, upon hearing Miss Alan's, "No," Augustus experiences an emotional response that automatically sends him into a state of physiological dysregulation and prohibits his ability to take in the entire verbal message. Augustus expresses his distress in tantrum behavior.

*When people are flooded they can't listen, even though
they might wish to. It's not anyone's fault that they can't
listen when flooded; it's a natural fight-or-flight response,
though operating a bit out of context.*

John Gottman

In the story, Augustus begins by dropping to the ground, kicking and screaming, to show his disagreement. As he becomes more emotionally compromised and confused by the different answers he is receiving, he escalates his behaviors to throwing materials then tipping over his desk.

These behaviors may have worked for him in the past to change the adult's response, thereby resulting in the desired answer Augustus is seeking, "Yes, let's go swimming now. I don't want you to be upset." On the other hand, the tantrums may have resulted in adult directed reprimands and punishment for his dangerous behavior. A reprimand that includes a punishment, "Tantrums don't earn you swimming. Bad boys must stay back in class," would further reinforce the negative association between the word, "No," and anxiety, thereby fortifying Augustus' habitually explosive response.

*We will usually give up behaviors
that don't work if we are capable of better ones.*

William Glasser

Fortunately, in the case of Augustus, Miss Leaky identified the issue and took charge of the communication repair by interjecting her message, "YES, SWIMMING, first work, then swimming." Instead of punishing the behavioral outburst or even acknowledging it, Miss Leaky remained steadfast in her communication. Further, Miss Leaky did not allow Augustus' behavioral episodes to get him to the pool without finishing his work. While she chose to assist him in the end, Miss Leaky was firm in her resolve that he complete one activity before earning the other. Persisting with the request will habituate Augustus to realizing that the expectations Miss Leaky expresses will be constant, and his engaging in tantrum behavior will not work to hasten the delivery of his longings. Therefore, this habit of behavioral outbursts will decrease over time, as it will no longer work to satisfy Augustus' desires.

Relationship Dynamics

The degree of social cohesion that you feel with other people is the greatest predictor of success during a time of challenge and stress.

One Day University

Miss Leaky's actions served to provide Augustus a fulfillment of his communicative and psychological needs. Miss Leaky utilized a communication style with which Augustus is accustomed. She spoke in a short, pre-trained phrase he could process. She further focused her interaction with him to the issues of work and swimming. By doing so, she did not allow his tantrum to change the topic to his, "bad behavior," or to the accuracy of his work. Miss Leaky also supported Augustus' emotional state by encouraging his work, genially responding to his repeated questioning, and breaking-in when she realized Miss Alan's message was causing him distress. These components assist in developing attunement and trust between Augustus and Miss Leaky. As this is not the first time Miss Leaky and Augustus have engaged in interactions developing attunement, Augustus feels a sense of social cohesion that allows him to seek her out for reassurance. Since Augustus trusts Miss Leaky, he is able to recover from his tantrums relatively quickly and become amenable to her requests to finish his work.

Colette McNeil

Chapter 4
No Thank You

No. Uh-uhh. Nah. Nope. No way. Ew, not me! While there are many ways to refuse an offer, there is a common phrase taught which is considered polite. "No, thank you," is the universally acceptable response for cordially rejecting something offered. While slang is acceptable during informal interactions, the courteous approach is best in mixed company and formal settings. For children with autism, the variability of slang language makes their experience of the world much more confusing. Teaching one consistent expression that will be correct and appropriate regardless of the social context better supports children with autism.

HARU

One Morning in a Kindergarten Class
for Students with Autism

"Haru is passing out a special snack choice. When he comes to you, please practice your polite phrases by saying, 'Yes, please,' or, 'No, thank you.'" Miss Leaky hands Haru the box his mom sent to school.

Approaching Miss Leila and Jeffry, Haru reaches out to offer Jeffry the treat.

As Jeffry grasps the item, Miss Leila prompts, "Yes, please."

Imitating, "Yes, please," Jeffry takes the treat.

Miss Leila also agrees, "Yes please."

Haru moves on to a table with Nikki, Keith, and Travis. As Haru holds out the snack, Nikki shouts, "NO!"

Haru freezes, feeling condemned. Unsure, he reaches the item out again and Nikki strongly protests, "No! I don't want it. NO!"

The firm, "No," fills Haru with angst. *Thump*, his bottom hits the floor. He slumps over and cries.

Miss Leaky reminds Nikki, "Your language is, 'No, thank you.'" Speaking the phrase smoothly to give it a distinctly different auditory flow from the harsh, "No," Miss Leaky instructs Nikki to practice the phrase. Miss Leaky then encourages Haru to continue in his task, persuading him that he is okay, he is not in trouble, and he does not need to be sad.

Keith happily accepts the offer and is mindful to use his words, "Yes, please."

Travis doesn't want any, and as he gestures to push the item away, Miss Leaky models, "No, thank you."

"No, thank you," comes his echo.

Amiably moving to Mr. Randy's group, Haru holds out the item to Eduardo. "Yes, please!" Eduardo excitedly proclaims.

Mr. Randy is assisting Eva to get situated in her seat and absentmindedly waves off Haru, "No."

Haru pushes the item towards Mr. Randy again, and Mr. Randy responds a little louder, "No."

Feeling admonished, Haru drops to the floor and weeps.

"Oh, Mr. Randy forgot his polite phrase," comments Miss Leaky as she assists Haru to his feet. "It's ok," with a lilt in her voice and evenness of flow, she models, "No, thank you."

Mr. Randy replies, "Oh sorry. No, thank you, Haru."

Haru hands a treat to Otis who, mimicking Mr. Randy, pushes the treat away, "No."

Haru sits on the floor once more, this time screaming out and kicking his feet.

Miss Leaky corrects Otis, "Better language is, 'No, thank you.'" Providing support, Miss Leaky and Haru repeat the offer to Otis.

Modeling the proper phrase, Mr. Randy prompts, "No, thank you."

"No, thank you," cedes Otis.

Haru makes his offer to Eva, who refuses the item repeating after Mr. Randy's model, "No, thank you."

Agreeably, Haru moves on to the last table with Miss Zelda, Jacob and Larry.

Miss Zelda models her polite phrase for Jacob and Larry, "Yes, please."

Jacob accepts, "Yes, please."

"No, yuck, no!" Larry pushes the item away.

"Ahhhh!" Haru falls to the floor yet again.

Miss Leaky instructs Larry to use better language and encourages Haru to try again. Holding out the item to Larry, Haru extends his offer.

Larry complies with Miss Leaky's coaching, "No, thank you."

Contented, Haru turns away from Larry and toward Miss Leaky, holding out a serving for her.

Smiling, Miss Leaky responds gently, "No, thank you."

Beaming back, Haru looks around the room to see if there is anyone he missed. Miss Leaky praises Haru for his efforts and tells him he may have his snack. Placing the box of goodies on the counter, Haru serves himself and takes his place at the table. Opening the package, Haru inhales deeply, enjoying the sweet fragrance. Biting down slowly and deliberately, he delights in the opportunity to eat his favorite treat.

Breaking it Down

Communication

As discussed in previous chapters, "No," tends to be an emotionally charged word that can set off an undesirable reaction in children with autism. In Haru's story, Miss Leaky is teaching the students to use, "No, thank you," as a common response when refusing an offered item. She is purposefully saying the phrase using a soft and light tone and saying the words in smooth succession, without any pause between the *no* and *thank you*. Carefully teaching the short phrase in this manner ensures that the expression is heard and processed as an auditory language chunk that holds a specific meaning separate from a short, "No." As Haru progresses through the groups offering his treats, his emotional state remains calm and cheerful with the predictable, "Yes, please" and, "No, thank you," responses. When he hears a harsh, "No," from some of his classmates and Mr. Randy, he immediately interprets the word not as a simple refusal of the snack item but as a reproach for making the offer. Haru is confused and expresses his habitual anxious response by dropping to the floor and crying.

Supplementary Influences

Words have enormous power.
The wrong word has led to wars...

Susan David

When Miss Leaky and staff teach and use consistent verbal language that is supportive of the needs of Haru, his anxious emotions are quelled. Haru can comprehend his expectations and produce an appropriate response within a predictable context. When Nikki, Mr. Randy, Otis and Larry deviate from the script, Haru is easily confused and believes he is being reprimanded. He quickly becomes agitated and responds with emotional distress. As Miss Leaky supports Haru and insists on the use of the appropriate responses from his classmates, Haru is reinforced and recovers quickly from his angst. In the *SCERTS Model - a Comprehensive Educational approach for Children with Autism Spectrum Disorders (Volume II, Program Planning and Intervention)*, "Transactional Supports," are identified as key components of purposeful engagement with children with autism. Transactional supports are those efforts provided by the child's partners to promote learning and development. Providing predictable routines, using specifically scripted language in short phrases, and framing activities with consistent content and context are some ways of facilitating improved comprehension for children with autism. "Transactional Support, Interpersonal Support," is discussed as the need for the child's partner to be specific about what their responsibilities are within the social exchange. When we adults become more aware of the needs of the children, we can better identify which words and actions accomplish purposeful, positive engagement.

Colette McNeil

Relationship Dynamics

*Even the smallest shots of Positivity
can give someone a serious competitive edge.*

Shawn Achor

The limited expressive and receptive verbal language skills of children with autism often motivate adults to use and teach the simple word, "No," as a refusal strategy. These caring adults are attempting to be considerate of the child's limitations by teaching what appears to be the simplest answer. Unfortunately, the single word, "No," is also used in contemporary language to reprimand, request to stop an action, respond to a yes/no question, identify that something is not correct and indicate the absence of an item. These multiple meanings of, "No," are confusing to a child with autism. Therefore, making the effort to use different wording for each definition of, "No," will give the children distinct meanings for each circumstance. Using the scripted language chunk, "No, thank you," teaches a clear refusal strategy and further benefits the child by training a delivery that is considered polite. Expressively, the child will be able to use this phrase in all contexts and will be affectionately admired by extended family, educators and community members for the cordial and mannered response. This admiration will go a long way in keeping the affect surrounding the child positively skewed. Positivity is a catalyst for open and pleasant social engagement.

Chapter 5
No Cookies

DENNIS

Standing in the kitchen, cabinet door open, Dennis and Dad are seeking a snack. "Well, Dennis, it looks like we need to make a trip to the store soon. We are out of your favorite items."

Holding his picture communication support device, Dennis requests cookies.

Dad shows Dennis a bag of crackers and a granola bar, "No cookies, how about one of these?" Dennis repeats his request for cookies and Dad replies, "No. No cookies."

A typical snack time in Dennis' house is usually pretty casual. Dennis may receive a package of whatever snack he wants as long as he uses his communication device to make the request. Following his training and routine, Dennis persists with his request for cookies, creating a picture sentence, "I want cookie, please."

Dad answers more firmly, "No cookies."

Feeling confused and reprimanded, Dennis becomes agitated, screams out and stomps his foot.

Opening the cupboard wider, Dad encourages Dennis to look inside, "Look Dennis, we have *NO* cookies."

Once Dennis inspects the cupboard and can't find cookies, he looks back at the pictures in his communication device and requests fish crackers.

Dad sighs and says, "sorry buddy, no fish crackers." Again, Dennis is confused by his dad's refusal and reiterates his request for fish crackers.

"No fish crackers," replies Dad, holding up raisins and a pack of nuts, "How about one of these?"

Dennis begins to whine and twist his body, threatening to tantrum. Dad once again opens the cupboard wider and picks Dennis up to see all the shelves, "Look, *NO* fish crackers."

Looking carefully around the cupboard, Dennis concedes that the fish crackers are missing. Scanning the pictures in his communication device, he next requests fruit snacks.

Dad is relieved to see a box of fruit snacks and pulls it off the shelf. As he reaches into the box, Dad's stomach tightens and a slight queasiness stirs. Desperately peering inside, Dad is hopeful that his eyes will find what his hand could not. Enveloped in disappointment, Dad's voice is compassionate, "Oh no buddy, the box is empty. No fruit snacks."

Hearing, "No," while looking at the box in his dad's hand launches Dennis into emotional tumult. He drops his communication device, screams with fury, and striking his dad, grabs for the box.

Permitting Dennis to snatch the empty box, Dad sympathizes, "I know, I know. I'm frustrated too. The box is empty. There are *NO* fruit snacks!"

Unable to find a pack of fruit snacks in the box, Dennis drops to the floor and cries.

After giving Dennis a few minutes to cry-it-out, Dad engages Dennis one last time. Wishing to pacify Dennis and provide him an agreeable treat without further emotional outbursts, Dad takes away Dennis' communication device and, lifting him once more, encourages Dennis to make a choice, "What do you want?"

Dennis looks around, considers his options, then picks a package of cheese and crackers. Dad takes a package for himself and two boxes of juice. The pair enjoy their snack together.

Breaking it Down

Communication

PRAGMATICS
The branch of linguistics concerned with meaning in context, or the meanings of sentences in terms of the speaker's intentions in using them

Webster's New World College Dictionary

In the saga of Dennis, there are many encouraging factors at play that support communication between Dennis and Dad. The two are engaged in a predictable routine activity. Dennis has the use of an alternative communication device to assist in making requests. Realizing the lack of snack items available, Dad is engaging Dennis in an empathetic manner and offering alternative choices. Finally, Dad ultimately changes from the requirement to request with the communication device to picking from the real objects available.

The struggle in our illustration falls on the common communication strategy Dad uses to inform Dennis that the items he is requesting are unavailable. "No cookies, no fish crackers, no fruit snacks," are all typical comments for many people. The difficulty for Dennis is that his lack of pragmatic language conception due to his autism keeps him from determining if the, "No," is meant as a refusal of the item, an admonishment for requesting the item, or an indication that the item is not available. Since, it is Dennis' perception that, "No," is more often used as a reprimand or request to stop doing something, he interprets the information Dad is providing as a rebuke. This perceived criticism by Dad is upsetting to Dennis because the predictable routines of snack time in Dennis' home give Dennis the expectation that he is able to receive the item he wants when he asks for it using his communication device. Therefore, Dennis interprets Dad's, "No," not only as a reprimand, but also as a deviation from the understood rules of snack.

Moving forward, Dennis's family could decide to change the interaction altogether by allowing Dennis to request from only a small sample of choices shown to him. This strategy would avoid the issue of communicating the absence of something. If this is the stage of comprehension at which Dennis functions best, it is a good choice. But, if Dennis is further along in his comprehension skills and the issue is more a matter of vocabulary versus concept, then I encourage Dennis' family to consider modifying their verbal phrasing. Dennis will encounter many opportunities in life when desired items are unavailable, and the ability to understand the communicated response will benefit Dennis for the long term.

I have heard families and educators replace, "No cookies," with, "All gone," "Finished," "Zero left," and, "Not a choice." The specific phrase Dad chooses to begin using with Dennis will depend on several factors. In deciding the best wording for Dennis's family, Dad could consider the length of phrase that Dennis is able to comprehend and what expression makes sense within the family dynamics. He would benefit from collaborating with Dennis' school so that the language used is consistent across environments. Further, Dennis' team would gain an advantage from considering how words and phrases are already being used to communicate other concepts to him. For instance, "Finished," is often used to let children know an activity is over and a transition will occur; and "Zero," is a math term that will be used when learning numbers and math concepts. I personally like the phrases, "All gone," or, "Not a choice," and I encourage families and educators to consider this issue carefully.

Supplementary Influences

A Note on Behaviors

Behavioral outbursts that include physical acting out are issues of concern. It is important to teach children not to throw items or assault others when they are upset. In many circumstances, a direct focus on engaging in strategies to address and correct the inappropriate behaviors would be proper. Compassionate understanding of a child's emotional distress is commendable, yet it does not alleviate the responsibility of the adult to consistently communicate expectations of appropriate behavioral interactions. Proper behavior training is extremely important for children with autism. Negative, inappropriate behaviors easily become habits that are not naturally outgrown for the autistic child. A teenaged or adult person with autism who engages in violent behaviors is not only dangerous to him/herself and others but is severely limited in opportunities for educational, social, and vocational arrangements, regardless of his/her intellectual abilities.

Colette McNeil

When you resolve conflict effectively, you are trusted.
If you are soft on people and tough on issues,
you don't bruise egos or make enemies.
That inspires others to negotiate fairly.

Mel Silberman

In our particular tale, Dad chose to refrain from punitively reacting to Dennis' outburst. Part of a good behavior management plan is knowing when the interactions of the caregiver are contributing to the behavioral disruption. If adults can identify the language breakdown issue and remain focused on improving communication, versus being derailed into reacting to the behavioral outburst, then communication will improve, the child's anxiety will be alleviated and the behavioral component will correct itself.

When engaging children with autism, it is fundamental to remain focused on one expectation at a time. In our account, Dad did not reprimand Dennis for dropping his communication device or hitting. He afforded Dennis some time to recover from his distress and stayed focused on the communication breakdown. That said, if the outburst becomes overtly dangerous, then stopping all instructional engagement and protecting for safety until the child has recovered would be the appropriate response. After a recovery, returning to the interaction with a plan of improved communication will reinforce the concept that desires can be satisfied when behaviors are cooperative. Dad achieved this by allowing Dennis to pick from the available items in the cupboard. Further, Dad avoided a common error of trying to appease Dennis by simply giving him a snack item while he displayed tantrum behaviors. If this error had occurred, Dennis may have learned to exhibit disruptive behaviors to gain his desires. Dad's response to allow Dennis a few minutes to recover, and to remain calm, compassionate and focused on improving the communication was exactly the intervention needed.

Relationship Dynamics

The ratio of positive to negative affect during conflict in stable relationships is 5:1

John Gottman

Dennis' father is relating to him in a sympathetic manner but is having difficulty helping Dennis understand that the, "No," he is using is describing the absence of the requested snack items and is not an admonishment. Dennis is becoming upset, so Dad develops a strategy to help Dennis understand. While the verbal exchange is troubled, Dad's efforts to aid Dennis, by ultimately removing the picture communication support and allowing Dennis to simply pick a snack item from the available packages, assists the two in getting through the arduous moment. Relationship researcher John Gottman describes in his book, *The Science of Trust: Emotional Attunement for Couples,* a concept of "Positive Sentiment Override." Essentially, the theory explains that when individuals engage with each other in a manner that is more often positive, by a factor of at least 5 positive interactions to 1 negative interaction, "the positive sentiments we have about the relationship and our partner override negative things our partner might do." Gottman further describes that this is, "where trust has its big payoff. In a trusting relationship, even an event as simple as our partner's handholding can downregulate our activated fight-or-flight state." In our story, Dennis' emotions are dysregulated because he does not comprehend his father's, "No," and he is disquieted by a change in the predictable rules of snack at home. But, he is easily calmed when Dad attempts to help him understand by changing the communicative interaction. After Dad picks up Dennis to see for himself what is in the cupboard, Dennis is able to ascertain that the desired items are not available. Dad's change in strategy assists Dennis to down-regulate his emotional angst and continue engaging. Dad and Dennis clearly have a strong relationship. Improving the conceptual communication of *not available/all-gone/not-a-choice* may additionally enhance this strong relationship by eluding future breakdowns in communication.

Chapter 6
Is this a Dog?

Asking yes/no questions is straight forward, right? *Yes, it is,* or, *No, it is not.* What could be the problem with the question, "Is this a dog?"

The conceptual understanding of *is/is not, same/different, belongs/does not belong, equal/not equal* are routine lessons in school. Starting in preschool, matching objects, and moving through graduate school, identifying complexities of math expressions and intricate science categories, the concept is integral to a broad spectrum of knowledge. The lesson of identifying what is *in/out* of a category is pertinent, yet many times the instructional approach and verbal explanation can unintentionally make the learning experience more complicated than needed for a child with autism.

Jacob

"Look here, Jacob. What do you see?"

"Dog."

"Good. Now let's find the same in this line." Miss Edna points to the pictures on the first line of the worksheet and models the lesson.

"Is this a dog? No. It's a Cat." Miss Edna crosses out the cat.

"Is this a dog? No. It's a chicken." Miss Edna places an X on the chicken.

"Is this a dog? No. It's a rabbit." Miss Edna marks out the rabbit.

"Is this a dog? Yes. It's a dog. See? It's the same as the first picture. Make a circle around it." Miss Edna helps Jacob draw a circle around the dog. "Now you do the next line."

Miss Edna asks, "Look here. What do you see?"

Jacob replies, "Rabbit."

"Yes, it is a rabbit. Now let's find the picture that is the same. Look at the pictures. Is this a rabbit?

Jacob draws a circle around the picture of the cow.

"No. That is a cow. We only want the same as the first one. Cow is not the same. Cross it out." Miss Edna helps Jacob cross out the cow picture. "Okay, now we are looking for a rabbit like this one." Miss Edna points to the first picture in the line. Pointing then to the third picture, which is a mouse, "Is this a rabbit?"

Jacob repeats, "Rabbit," and begins to draw a circle.

"No. It's a mouse. Cross it out."

Indicating the fourth picture, Miss Edna questions, "Is this a rabbit?"

"Rabbit," replies Jacob.

"Yes, rabbit. Make a circle." Pointing to the last picture, "Is this a rabbit?"

Jacob begins making a circle, "Rabbit."

"No. Pig. Cross it out. Not the same."

The worksheet on same versus different has Jacob stressed, and he begins weeping. Miss Edna, recognizing Jacob's frustration, cajoles, "It's okay. I will help you. Come on, Jacob. You know your animals. Let's try the next line. What is this animal?"

Jacob answers, "Pig."

"Yes. Good. Now look at this picture. Is it a pig?"

"Pig," echoes Jacob.

"No."

Whining, Jacob squirms in his chair.

"Jacob, what animal is this?"

"Dog."

"Yes. Very good. It is a dog. Dog is not a pig, not the same. Make an X."

Jacob crosses off the dog picture as he is instructed.

Miss Edna points to the next picture, "Is this a pig?"

Jacob sits quietly, looking for more instruction from Miss Edna.

"Jacob, what animal is this?"

"Pig."

"Yes, very good!" Pointing back and forth between both pig pictures, "See, pig and pig. They are the same. Circle the pig."

Jacob circles the pig picture and repeats, "Pig."

"Okay, last picture. Is this a pig?"

Jacob again sits quiet. He watches carefully for Miss Edna to give him the answer.

"Jacob, what animal is this?"

"Chicken."

"Yes, good. It's a chicken. Is it a pig?"

"Chicken," replies Jacob.

"No. It is not a pig. Make an X."

At the annunciation of Miss Edna's, "No," Jacob again becomes weepy.

Agitated, Jacob makes his mark over the picture of the chicken as directed then drops his pencil, places his head in his arms and lays them on the desk.

"Okay, okay, I know that was hard. Good trying, Jacob. Let's take a break. It's time for recess."

BREAKING IT DOWN

Seek first to understand, then to be understood.

Stephen R. Covey

Communication

Jacob knows his animals and Miss Edna is walking Jacob through each step of the work sheet, yet this lesson is confusing and stressful for Jacob. One could extrapolate that Jacob does not understand the concept of *same/different, is/is not.* But, is the trouble with the concept or the verbal exchange?

The wearisome instructional experience outlined above is common amongst many educators and students with autism. The worksheet is relatively simple, and if explained from a different approach, Jacob could better show his understanding and competency. The lesson focus is asking the learner to identify the same picture as the first in the line. This is a lesson on *sameness.* When Miss Edna spends time and lengthy verbal expressions alerting Jacob to what is *not the same,* she is talking Jacob into a downward emotional spiral. Of first concern is the length of her verbalizations and the abstract reasoning needed to identify what is *not* correct. Further, the repeated, "No," comments before identifying the incorrect pictures can be interpreted by Jacob as a reprimand as opposed to a simple communication of the lack of sameness with the first picture.

This worksheet could be taught with far less verbiage and result in far more success if Miss Edna were to focus solely on the specific positive concept of sameness. Instead of asking, "Is this a dog?" Miss Edna could ask Jacob to identify the first animal in the line, asking, "What is this?"

Jacob, knowing his animals, would answer, "Dog."

Miss Edna could then simply say, "Find same," speaking only the purposeful lesson vocabulary. She could model the first line by pointing to the first picture and saying, "Dog, find same," then point to the matching picture, saying, "Dog." Next, pointing between the two pictures, Miss Edna could state, "Dog, dog, SAME." After instructing Jacob to circle the matching picture, Miss Edna would encourage Jacob to complete the rest of the lesson. Miss Edna could support Jacob by using only the limited targeted vocabulary, "What's this?" and, "Find same." When Jacob realizes he simply needs to use his visual strength to scan the line for the matching picture, he could finish the worksheet independently. Teaching the repeated targeted vocabulary, "Same," will assist Jacob in understanding the expectations in future lessons when asked to find the *same* item, sort by the *same* attribute, identify items that belong in the *same* categories, etc. Further, avoiding the use of the word, "No," when identifying each of the *not-same* or *different* items, will completely avoid any opportunity for Jacob to misinterpret Miss Edna's intentions.

Supplementary Influences

The TEACCH (**T**eaching **E**ducation of **A**utistic and related **C**ommunication **H**andicapped **Ch**ildren) program training discusses the importance of understanding the unique characteristics of children with autism. TEACCH trainers discuss an idea of a "Culture of autism," being the communal characteristics of children with autism that requires a different approach to instruction in order to elicit the best results. When teaching children with autism, thoughtfully structuring the environmental, communicative, and instructional focus of the program heightens student outcomes.

One commonly exhibited characteristic of children with autism is restricted thought processing. Children with autism are concrete thinkers. They typically understand literal concepts related to tangible objects and observable actions that can be specifically labeled. Ideas that require theoretical thoughts and the ability to reference non-tangible and non-observable ideas are abstract and often incomprehensible to children with autism. "Yes/no," questions are generally abstract ideas that are difficult for children with autism to conceptualize. With specific training, children can learn to respond to, "Do you want," questions with, "Yes/no," answers, but other questions, such as, "Is this a—," "Do you feel—," "Do you like—," continue to be very difficult concepts to grasp. Further, the varied notions being addressed in these questions add to the confusion of a child with autism when trying to understand the exact word/idea correlation. Adults who choose to reconsider what information the, "Yes/no," question is trying to accomplish and address the issue in a more concrete manner will communicate more effectively with their children.

Relationship Dynamics

*It simply makes no difference how good the rhetoric is
or even how good the intentions are;
if there is little or no trust,
there is no foundation for permanent success.*

Stephen R. Covey

In the story of Jacob, Miss Edna is engaging, compassionate, patient, and encouraging. She is working hard to explain the lesson and support Jacob, yet Jacob becomes frustrated and weepy. In Chapter 5, I discussed how John Gottman's explanation of Positive Sentiment Override supports a positive relationship that allows partners to overcome intermittent negative interactions. Gottman also discusses the reverse of Positive Sentiment Override as, "Negative Sentiment Override." He states, "In negative sentiment override, the negative sentiments we have about the relationship and our partner override anything positive our partner might do." It is an unfortunate reality that many children with autism appear to unwittingly fall into a state of negative sentiment override with adults due to their lack of social communication skills and abstract reasoning.

The hazards in the story of Jacob occur regularly and repeatedly in many instructional interactions. In Jacob's case, he is finding Miss Edna's approach hard to follow, confusing, and overwhelming. Miss Edna's positive intentions fail to support Jacob's anxiety because Jacob is unable to grasp Miss Edna's conceptions. Jacob expresses frustration, confusion, and sadness due to this interaction with Miss Edna. Miss Edna and Jacob are not engaged in conflict, yet Jacob is experiencing negative emotions. Adults are well meaning, yet often the common language used during instruction leaves learners with autism experiencing heightened negative sentiments towards their instructors. A high level of tantrum behavior due to seemingly non-issues could be an indication of a child's Negative Sentiment Override.

In his book, *The Quality School, Managing Students without Coercion*, William Glasser shares that, "teaching is difficult under the best of circumstances," and goes on to point out, "The failure to take into account the needs of the student... can make the job almost impossible." Failure to take into account the essential aspects of autism amplifies this sentiment. Interactions with youth will continue to be needlessly strained until adults become conscientious of the pitfalls in common verbiage. As grownups learn to speak in a manner that simplifies the verbal gobbledygook and speak directly to what the expectation *is* versus *is not*, children can begin to have better comprehension, de-stress, and experience higher rates of positive interactions.

If Miss Edna chooses to change her approach as outlined above when teaching future lessons, she will be tapping in to Jacob's strengths by focusing lessons on the concrete concepts that Jacob can grasp, allowing him to rely on his visual skills to take in information and supporting his auditory processing weakness by teaching minimal, specific verbiage. Jacob's ability to better comprehend the expectations would instill feelings of self-confidence and trust towards Miss Edna.

Chapter 7
NO! Stop! NO!

Machoa

Reaching into the back seat to collect her shopping bags, Mom holds on tight to Machoa's arm.

Leaning away, wiggling his bottom, twisting and turning, 4-year-old Machoa whines and fusses.

"Wait a minute, Machoa. Mommy just needs these bags."

Machoa responds to the sound of his mother's voice by performing his best twisting dead-man's drop. His bottom hitting the ground with a thud, he has managed to break free of the irritating grasp. With practiced precision, Machoa explodes to his feet and swiftly sprints through the parking lot toward the grocery store.

"NO! Stop! NO!" Reacting in panic, Machoa's mother breaks into a frightful chase, "Please no cars, please no cars, please no cars," she chants under her breath. Screaming again, "Machoa, NO!"

Thank goodness, Machoa makes it to the storefront unharmed as Mom catches up to him and takes him in her arms. Breathing heavily, Mom places Machoa in the shopping cart basket. He is a little too big for the cart now, but he will sit in the basket area and not run off—so in the cart he goes. Mom collects herself, organizes her items and takes a deep breath. Frazzled, but accustomed to such incidents, she presses on in her routines.

As the pair make their way through the grocery store, Machoa is happy and energetically flapping his hands. Mom places some canned vegetables in the cart with him and he holds a can, feeling its cool tin. In the produce section, Mom is inspecting some oranges when Machoa jumps to his feet and takes an orange from the bottom tier.

"No. Stop." Mom is too late to catch his little hand as several oranges tumble to the floor. "No, Machoa. That's not okay." Mom helps Machoa sit down in the basket and lets him hold his orange while she retrieves the fallen fruit. Machoa remains joyful and seems content.

Down the breakfast aisle, Mom is showing Machoa several boxes of cereal and offering him some choices. Machoa picks Fruity Rings. Mom hands the box to him then, stepping a couple feet away, replaces the other package. As she glances towards the cart, Mom is surprised to find Machoa leaning over the edge reaching for something on the shelf. The cart is listing slightly as Machoa lingers precariously over the side.

"No! No!" Mom rushes and catches Machoa, placing him back in the cart. "Machoa, sit down."

Ignoring his mother, Machoa lunges forward, reaching towards a box of Cinnamon Squares. Holding Machoa back from falling, his mother hands him the box of cereal and places him in a seated position in the basket. Machoa holds the box close to his face, gazing intently at the picture.

Mom and Machoa work their way through the grocery store and get checked-out with no further incidents. Exiting the store, Machoa fusses to be let out of the cart. Mom is reluctant to let him walk through the parking lot today, as he has been very active and she wants to keep him safe.

Machoa appeals strongly to be released from his confinement, and as soon as Mom stops the cart next to the car, he hastens to his feet and begins bouncing energetically. Deciding it would be safest to secure Machoa into his car seat before unloading the groceries, Mom accedes to his insistence. Lifting him from the cart, she stands him between herself and the open door for just a second as she moves his stuffed toy from the seat.

Diving past her legs, Machoa jettisons himself toward the parking lot.

Responding quickly with a grasp of Machoa's shirt, "No! Stop! No!" Mom's voice sounds alarmingly. Machoa struggles, but Mom is able to swiftly place him in the car and securely buckle his seatbelt.

Another deep breath, groceries loaded, Mom and Machoa drive home.

Breaking it Down

Communication

The shopping trip with Machoa and Mom is riddled with frightful moments. Mom is doing a good job of keeping her composure in the face of some difficult and fearful circumstances. She is using concise and direct verbiage and she is attending diligently to Machoa. Mom's words and actions are just as they should be under the circumstances. The only trouble with the interaction is that Machoa is not responding at all to Mom's verbal expressions. As he runs quickly through the parking lot, he does not stop until Mom catches up to him. Pulling down the oranges, Machoa, unaffected by Mom's reprimand, remains joyful and engaged with his orange. When leaning precariously over the edge of the cart, and later attempting to run from Mom at the car, Machoa is only responsive to Mom's touch and physical assists to sit.

I bet you are thinking, *Well, this is autism.* I agree this *is* autism, or at least the type of experiences many families undergo. I propose that this is why an emergency "NO!" response must be specifically and diligently taught. In our story, Machoa makes no connection between his mother's voice and an expectation of him. In these examples, Mom's voice is of no more concern to him than other sounds in the environment such as the cars driving by, the wheels of the shopping cart, other people talking, the music being played in the store, etc. A correlation between Mom's voice speaking, "No!" and an expectation for Machoa to stop all motion as rapidly as possible will need to be purposefully trained. I realize this message is counter to the previous chapters, within which I have encouraged adults to find replacement verbiage to the word, "No." It is my experience and observation that when the adult's alarm and panic ridden protective, fight or flight mode kicks in, the only words produced are those deeply ingrained and practiced. An alarmed, "No," will override any mindfully learned phrase. Therefore, teaching to this panicked, "No," is prudent. Don't fight nature; adjust your instruction to align with instinct.

When challenges loom and we get overwhelmed,
our rational brains can get hijacked by emotions.

Shawn Achor

Teaching Machoa to respond to Mom's, "No," will require planned instructional situations set up in controlled environments. Mom will need to say the word, "No," in a firm tone and physically assist Machoa to pull his hands to his body and freeze all motion. There should be no reprimand or punishment accompanying this training. The emphasis is not to indicate that Machoa is being naughty. The purpose is to consistently and persistently teach that Machoa will be expected to halt all motion and not touch anything near him. For Machoa, the *what-to-do* correlation when hearing, "No," is *freeze.* Praise and other positive reinforcement can be provided for Machoa's appropriate responses. As the training progresses, Machoa will be given the, "No," command without the physical prompt to freeze his motion, then from a short distance and increasingly further distances until Machoa is able to comply from at least across a room. Machoa would benefit from parents, extended family, teachers, therapists, and caregivers, all working on this instruction simultaneously so that he can learn the short and pronounced sound, "No," has meaning and can generalize its intent across people and environments.

Supplementary Influences

Our species has evolved a
physiological defense response that
Hans Selye called the "general alarm response."
This response takes over when we perceive danger.

John M. Gottman

Promoter of visual strategies for autism Barbara Bloomfield teaches in her *Icon to I Can* presentations that children with autism are less able to respond to a command to, "Stop," when they are running. She explains children with autism respond better to directions, such as, "come here," or, "turn around," as these instructions allow the students to maintain their physical motion while altering the direction of travel in an effort to comply. The command to, "Stop," is asking for both compliance to an instruction and the effort to halt the physical momentum, which is a more difficult process. I agree with her point and believe this vocabulary change can be integrated into habitual instructional practices. Another strategy I have seen parents and teachers effectively use with their children is a command to, "Sit down," in order to stop an unsafe action. I again find this to be a productive strategy within routine interactions. Both of these approaches give the children a specific action to complete and avoid the unnecessary use of a vague, "No." Yet, I encourage teaching the emergency, "No." This instruction will support the natural inclinations of adults when they are emotionally compromised by dangerous circumstances and revert to vocabulary that is spontaneously produced during an alarmed response.

Relationship Dynamics

In our story, Mom and Machoa have some strong predictable routines in place which keep Machoa generally in a well-regulated emotional state. Machoa knows to sit in the cart and responds well to Mom's reminders. Mom allows Machoa to hold items in the cart that are interesting to him and choose items he likes while shopping. Further, by electing to buckle Machoa into his car seat prior to putting the groceries away, she is attentive to his request to get out of the cart. As Mom chooses to work with Machoa in responding safely to, "No," she will experience fewer moments of anxiety due to Machoa's risky actions. This reduction in stress will allow for continued and likely improved positive relations between Mom and Machoa, as outings will be overall safer and more pleasant.

Chapter 8
No Talia

Alignment between words and actions
is just as important as consistency of behavior.
You might even argue that they are the same,
especially since 'what you do' and
'what you say' are both behaviors.

Harold Hillman

Talia

Monday:

"I want Cheetos."

"You don't have Cheetos today. Your mom sent you potato chips."

Reaching across the table, Talia repeats, "I want Cheetos."

"No, Talia, those are not your Cheetos."

"Cheetos! I want Cheetos!"

"No, you have chips."

Talia throws the chips on the ground, her voice raised and disquieted, "I want Cheetos!"

"No Cheetos. They belong to Harold." Picking up the bag of chips, Miss Edna encourages Talia to eat her own lunch.

"I want Cheetos!" Talia jumps up and, leaning across the table, grasps at Harold's Cheetos.

"No, Talia!"

Talia screams and lunges her body across the table.

Miss Edna reaches over and blocks Talia's attempts to steal the Cheetos. "This is not okay. Sit down."

Talia throws herself backwards off the bench and falls to the ground, kicking and screaming, "Cheeeee-toos!"

Students and staff eating in the cafeteria have begun staring watchfully at the commotion. Nervousness building within her, Miss Edna becomes eager to calm Talia and reduce the dramatics of the scene she is creating. "Harold, can you share your Cheetos? Here, you like chips, don't you?" Miss Edna gives Harold half of Talia's chips and takes half of Harold's Cheetos. Harold does not protest and enjoys his offered trade.

Miss Edna shows two Cheetos to Talia, "Okay. Okay, Talia. Look, here are some Cheetos."

Talia reaches for the Cheetos and Miss Edna pulls them back, "Sit at the table."

Talia jumps up and is instantly smiling and relaxed as she sits at the table.

Miss Edna puts the handful of Cheetos she traded with Harold on a napkin next to the half empty bag of chips, "There, happy now? You don't need to throw a fit."

Appeased, Talia eats her lunch without any further incidents.

Tuesday:

"Well, what did you bring for lunch today, Talia? I see a sandwich, and look, you have Cheetos! How nice. What do you have, Frank? Yum, a sandwich and carrots. Oh, you have fruit snacks. What a treat!"

"I want fruit snacks," interjects Talia.

"Those are Frank's fruit snacks. Look, you have Cheetos today, and your favorite apple juice. Here, I will open your Cheetos," Miss Edna tries to distract Talia from her attention to Frank's fruit snacks.

"I want fruit snacks!" Talia screams boisterously and lunges across the table.

Miss Edna was not expecting Talia's quick movements and is unable to react quickly enough to block Talia from snatching the bag.

Frank screams and reaches for his stolen package. Miss Edna quickly retrieves the item from Talia and returns it to Frank. Recruiting help from Miss Katy, Miss Edna encourages Frank to move further down the table, away from Talia.

Escalating her agitation, Talia flails her arms and drops to the floor, kicking and screaming, "Fruit snacks! Fruit snacks! Fruit snacks!"

"No, Talia. No fruit snacks. Maybe your mom can send some tomorrow."

Talia's screams get louder, and she tries kicking Miss Edna's legs.

"She can have my fruit snacks."

Miss Edna turns to find a boy from the third-grade class seated behind her, holding out a package of fruit snacks. "Oh, that is so nice of you, but your mom sent those for you."

"It's okay. I have two packs. I want to share." Stretching the package towards Talia, "Here you go. Have my fruit snacks."

Talia grabs the packet, climbs back on the bench and reaching up to Miss Edna, evenly requests, "I want open."

Colette McNeil

Opening the package for Talia, Miss Edna expresses her gratitude to the young man, "That was very generous of you! Thank you. You made her very happy."

Talia shoves the fruit snacks in her mouth in rapid succession. The boy smiles and turns back around to talk with his friends.

Wednesday:

"Talia, let's have you sit here at the end of the table today." Frank and Harold are seated at the other end of the table. Miss Edna is hopeful that strategically seating Talia with fewer peers surrounding her may help diminish the temptation to want what others have. There is a space left directly across from and to the side of Talia.

Helping Talia explore her lunch items, Miss Edna ingratiatingly engages, "Wow Talia, look, fish crackers, a banana, and juice. You are a lucky girl." Talia begins eating her lunch and Miss Edna is hopeful to have found a solution to Talia's tantrums.

"I want cookie." Holding up his cookies, Lee, sitting to the right of Talia, asks for help opening his package.

Miss Katy opens Lee's cookies and, reaching to hand them back, exclaims, "Yum, chocolate chip."

Like a flash of lightening, Talia thrusts her body through the empty space between her and Lee, juts her arm across Lee's body and knocks him into Miss Katy. As Talia seizes the package of cookies, the table is accosted by her screeching, "Cookie! Want Cookie!" As quickly as she approached, Talia retreats to her seat, clutching tightly to the cookies.

Miss Edna grasps Talia's hands, narrowly preventing the first cookie from entering Talia's mouth. Screaming and struggling, Talia kicks and hits at Miss Edna. Miss Edna hands Miss Katy the cookie package, minus the one

Talia had in her hand. Miss Katy places herself between Lee and Talia. Soothing Lee's distress, she gives him back his cookies.

Miss Edna waits for Talia to settle down enough to respond to instruction. Showing Talia the cookie, Miss Edna instructs, "Use your language," then models, "I want cookie, please."

Crying, Talia repeats, "I want cookie, please." Shoving the one cookie in her mouth, Talia commands again, "I want cookie, please," and looks towards Lee.

Miss Katy presents Talia the empty package, "All gone."

Talia turns to her lunch items and settles in for an otherwise quiet meal.

Thursday:

Talia is once again strategically seated with some space between herself and her classmates. Miss Katy sits between Talia and the next student. "We have a special lunch today. Everyone is having pizza." Miss Edna carries a tray of plates with pizza slices. She hands the first plate to Frank, the second one to Lee and turns towards Talia, who has jumped up from her seat, dropped to the floor, and begun crying loudly and pounding her feet on the ground.

Miss Edna questions, "What now?! Talia, what do you want?"

Talia exclaims, "Pizza!"

"Yes, Talia. Your pizza is right here!" Frustrated, Miss Edna places a plate on the table.

Looking up, Talia, collects her emotions, returns to her seat and enjoys her pizza.

Friday:

Talia and Miss Katy are sitting next to each other at the end of the table as they had done on Thursday. Today seems to be going well and Talia is happy eating her lunch. Fridays are special because the students get a popsicle after finishing their meal. As Miss Edna gets out the box of popsicles, she comments to Miss Katy, "I will give Talia hers first."

Miss Katy begins to prompt Talia to request the Popsicle, but Miss Edna, not waiting for Talia's request, hands her the frozen treat, "I don't want another tantrum today." Talia accepts the popsicle with enthusiasm and remains calm throughout the meal.

BREAKING IT DOWN

Communication

Unfortunately, many times, "No," expressions lose their meanings when employed too often or without proper follow through during a denial response. When the meanings of words are not explicitly taught with consistency and direct correspondence to a specific action or object, children with autism are left to imagine their own implications and inevitably learn the wrong messages.

If a child hits and is told, "No," but hits again immediately after without adult intervention to stop the hitting, then the child learns that, "No," does not mean anything. "No," is just a sound the adult makes at random times or in response to the hit, as if striking a squeaky toy. What a fun game the child may play, pounding Daddy over and over to hear that noise, "No, no, no, no, no." Likewise, if a child begins to run towards the street and the frantic parent hollers, "NO!" but has not taught the freeze response, this child may perceive the loud vocalizations as excitement and run gleefully ahead.

In her book, *How to Use Power Phrases to Say What You Mean, Mean What You Say, & Get What You Want,* Meryl Runion shares:

> A 2002 survey by the Center for a New American Dream confirms how often "no" means "maybe." According to the survey, the average American child aged 12 to 17 will ask nine times for what he or she wants before the parents will give in. More than 12 percent of thirteen-year-olds admit to asking parents for what they want fifty times or more. Why? Because it works.

In the tale of Talia, the child is told, "No," to a request for other students' lunch items, but after the exhibition of crying and tantrum behavior, Talia is given the demanded items. Here, two incorrect messages have been taught to Talia. First the message is that, "No," means, "Maybe," and more likely, "Yes, but first you must *really show me you want it.*" Furthermore, it teaches Talia that the true communication Miss Edna is seeking from her is not the simple verbal request, but the crying and tantrum behavior. As you will notice in the story, each successive day Talia began to cry and tantrum quicker, more often, and to greater degrees. On Monday, she tried using her language several times before attempting to steal the Cheetos then dropping to the floor and screaming. By Thursday, Talia simply drops to the ground and tantrums without any verbal indication of her desires. Additionally, Miss Edna was already prepared to give Talia her slice of pizza and simply placed the plate on the table. Talia's perceived correlation is that because she screamed and kicked, she immediately received her pizza. Her speech and language training to make verbal requests has just been sabotaged. The communication rule Talia has learned is, *first cry and tantrum then get what you desire.*

> *Avoid saying anything you have no intent to follow-up on.*
> *Ask yourself, Do I really mean this?*
> *If I am tested, will I follow through?*

> *Meryl Runion*

Helping children understand that, "No," means, "You may not," is crucial. Using a language chunk as discussed in previous chapters, such as, "Not a choice," or, "Not for Talia," is an appropriate response within an intimate adult/ child relationship. Unfortunately, children are engaged with many adults throughout their lifetime that do not know how to use this more positive language to indicate a denial. Therefore, it is in the best interest of the child to teach them that the word, "No," means, "You may not." Coupling, "No," with a phrase, as describe above, is an appropriate approach to accomplish both intents. When a child asks for a desired interest, you can say, "No," then pause a few seconds and calmly state, "Not a choice." It is extremely important that adults consistently refuse to give-in or change their minds. At first, children may show a negative response to the adult's denial, but they will learn that inappropriate behaviors will not be rewarded. When denials are turned into admissions, the child learns that, "No," means, "Try harder. Show me you really want it by acting upset. Use different words, actions, etc." When adults are consistent about their, "No," and refrain from engaging the child in explanations, arguments, and changes of mind, then the word, "No," will become accepted. Consistent and persistent is the key. If you feel you may waiver, it is far better just to say, "YES," in the first place than to say, "No," and contribute to a lack of meaningful understanding.

Parents who are willing to suffer the pain
of the child's intense anger by firmly holding him
to the responsible course are teaching him
a lesson that will help him all his life.

William Glasser

If in future interactions Miss Edna chooses to remain firm in her denial, she will need to be patient with Talia's raised level of emotional distress during the first few occasions. It may be helpful for Miss Edna to practice her consistent, "No," within the classroom, where there are more supports, less distractions, and fewer opportunities for interactions from outside individuals. She could continue to set Talia up for success at lunch time by strategically seating Talia to avoid temptations and giving Talia her special items first. Then, as Talia learns to accept, "No," within a highly structured context, Miss Edna can generalize the expectations to multiple environments.

Supplementary Influences

In this chapter I am targeting the denial of a request. In previous chapters I have attempted to exemplify how, "No," has different meanings and encouraged the use of diverse vocabulary to communicate the varied meanings more clearly. I realize I am proposing that adults use the word, "No," as a means for a denial while I have also promoted the use of, "No," as an emergency freeze indication in Chapter 7. I do not believe these two uses are contradictory. If an adult says, "No," to a request for a cookie and the child freezes, then the adult has an opportunity to add a clarifying phrase, "Not a Choice." Further, if, "No," is used as an emergency freeze indication then the adult will also need to follow-up with an action or instruction to indicate what the child needs to do after freezing to remain safe such as, "Sit down." These two, "No," responses are compatible. Further, I have illustrated the use of the identical phrase, "Not a choice," as in Chapter 5, where Dennis was denied an item because it was not available. This statement remains appropriate under the circumstances of denial even though there are items available. Lunch items of the other students are, "Not a choice," for Talia. The underlying message remains the same—*the child may not have the requested item.*

Relationship Dynamics

I again highlight an appropriate excerpt from Meryl Runion's book *How to Use Power Phrases to Say What You Mean, Mean What You Say, & Get What You Want:*

> Do you ever say things you don't mean? For example, if you have kids, do you ever tell them to turn the television off and then ignore the fact that they haven't a half hour later? Then when you are finally serious about getting results, do you get angry? What happens when you do that is you teach people they don't have to pay attention to what you say until you get angry. You can avoid getting angry altogether by meaning what you say before you get angry. You set yourself up to get angry if that is the only time you mean your words.

When adults turn a denial into an admission after persistent complaints from a child with autism, they not only teach the wrong meaning of the word, "No," which will add to the child's anxiety, they may also become personally effected by negative emotions as Meryl Runion described. If both caregiver and child are experiencing these negative emotions, they are clearly not attuned to each other and the quality of their relationship is affected.

Among the most destructive of all our coercive practices is our overuse of personal criticism.

William Glasser

As we look back at our story of Talia, we can see some glimpses of Miss Edna beginning to show signs of frustration with Talia. On Monday, Miss Edna makes an undermining comment, "There, happy now? You don't have to throw a fit." On Thursday, Miss Edna's harsh comment, "What Now!" shows her rising level of agitation. Friday, Miss Edna gives Talia her treat first, but the emotional context is aggravated and avoidant of engaging the child. Talia is happy, but the educational arrangement of teaching Talia how to appropriately request items is also circumvented. The relationship between Talia and Miss Edna is declining and only Miss Edna can make a change in her words and actions to engender improvements. Talia is simply reacting to her interpretations of the environment and instinctively developing a strategy to get what she wants. She has no concept of the relationship or social components. If Miss Edna follows the advice of Meryl Runion, "Say what you mean and mean what you say without being mean when you say it," she will make great progress in building comprehension and a positive relationship with Talia.

Happiness is not the belief that we don't need to change; it is the realization that we can.

Shawn Achor

Colette McNeil

Chapter 9
Conclusion

Thank you for joining me on this journey through examining the stories of Corey, the students of Miss Leaky's class, Augustus, Haru, Dennis, Jacob, Machoa, and Talia. Exploring the layers of challenge within these teachable tales, I have illustrated situations when, "No," was unsuccessfully used to communicate the varied concepts of:

- Negating an action—"No Running"
- Using, "No," when the message is, "Yes/Later."
- Refusal of an offer—"No Thank You"
- Zero items available—"No Cookies"
- Abstract Yes/No questions—"Is this a Dog?"
- Emergency alarm response—Request to Freeze
- Denial of a request

The challenges illustrated within each of the stories are common everyday occurrences. Now I invite you to reflect upon how many of these circumstances could occur throughout a day in the life of a child with autism. If the child experiences each of the different, "No," concepts just once in any one day—that is seven separate frustrating and distressing episodes. That would be a very difficult day with multiple negative emotional experiences! If a child is exhibiting many episodes of tantrum behaviors daily, I encourage his/her guardians to pause and consider the vocabulary that is being used. A small change in verbiage could make a big impact on improving the interactions.

Within the explanations of the challenges found in each story, several underlying concepts for supporting children with autism were discussed:

- Take care to observe how common habitual language may be confusing to children with autism
- Say what *to-do* instead of what *not-to-do*
- Engage with children in structured, consistent, and predictable manners
- Reduce verbal output to simple short phrases
- Use consistent phrasing and language chunks to establish meaning
- Speak in concrete terms
- Change verbiage to communicate the positive expectation
- Take the time to specifically teach correlation between words and expectations
- Choosing to understand the needs and perceptions of children with autism and accepting the responsibility to change the way adults engage their individual child can improve trust, attunement and positive emotional relationships

It is my hope that exploring *Understanding the Challenges of -NO- for Children with Autism: Improving Communication - Increasing Positivity - Enhancing Relationships* has illuminated concepts that provoke reflection, promote discussion, and expand the awareness of parents, families, teachers, and caregivers. Embarking on the next steps towards making a change in your verbiage, I hearten adults to be kind to themselves and patient with the process. Change is a progression that starts with awareness but takes many transitional steps over time. I implore adults to pick one supporting concept that speaks to them and start there. Will you try to say what *to-do* more often, begin with teaching the emergency, "No," or simply begin observing your habitual verbal communication style? Only the individual person can know what approach will be best suited to his/her life. The key is making the choice to begin.

The ability to thoughtfully choose our vocabulary
when communicating with children with autism
resides within each of us and can result in
improving communication,
increasing positivity,
and enhancing relationships.

Colette McNeil

References

Abeckaser, D.A., Golombek, F., Melita, P., Robbins, I., Schoof, A., Singer, U. (Producers), & Michael A. (Director). (2015). *Experimenter:* (Motion Picture). United States: Magnolia Pictures

Achor, Shawn (2010-09-14). *The Happiness Advantage*: *The Seven Principles of Positive Psychology That Fuel Success and Performance at Work* (p. 14, 15, 17, 24, 48). The Crown Publishing Group. Kindle Edition.

Blank, M., McKirdy, L. S., & Payne, P. C. (2000). *Links to Language I & Links to Language II*. Blank, McKirdy, Payne.

Bloomfield, B.C. (2001). *Icon to I Can, a visual Bridge to Independence*. Presentation Materials.

Covey, Stephen R. (2013-11-15). *The 7 Habits of Highly Effective People: Powerful Lessons in Personal Change* (25th Anniversary Edition) (p. 74). RosettaBooks. Kindle Edition.

Cuddy, Amy (2015-12-22). *Presence: Bringing Your Boldest Self to Your Biggest Challenges* (p. 24). Little, Brown and Company. Kindle Edition.

Diagnostic and Statistical Manual of Mental Disorders, (Fifth Edition) (DSM-5) (2013). American Psychiatric Association (p. 31-32).

Frost, L. A., Bondy, A. S. (1994). *PECS The Picture Exchange Communication System, Training Manual*. Pyramid Educational Consultants, Inc.

Glasser MD, William (2010-11-16). *Choice Theory: A New Psychology of Personal Freedom* (p. 221). HarperCollins. Kindle Edition.

Glasser M.D., William (2010-11-16). *Quality School RI* (p. 24). HarperCollins. Kindle Edition.

Glasser MD, William (2013-03-19). *Take Charge of Your Life: How to Get What You Need with Choice-Theory Psychology* (p. 44). iUniverse. Kindle Edition.

Gottman, John M. (2011-05-09). *The Science of Trust: Emotional Attunement for Couples* (p. 19, 25, 32, 121, 143, 206, 208). W. W. Norton & Company. Kindle Edition

Gottman, John; Silver, Nan (2015-05-05). *The Seven Principles for Making Marriage Work: A Practical Guide from the Country's Foremost Relationship Expert* (Kindle Locations 533-534, 795-800, 808-812). Potter/TenSpeed/Harmony. Kindle Edition

Helmstetter, Dr. Shad (2011-06-09). *What To Say When You Talk To Your Self* (Kindle Locations 1825-1827). Park Avenue Press. Kindle Edition.

Hillman, Harold (2013-12-06). *The Impostor Syndrome: Becoming an Authentic Leader* (Kindle Locations 1237-1239). Random House New Zealand. Kindle Edition.

Leaf, R., McEachin, J. (1999). *A Work in Progress, Behavior Management Strategies and a Curriculum for Intensive Behavioral Treatment of Autism*. Autism Partnership.

Leaky, A. (2017, June). *One Summer Day in a Class for Elementary School Students with Autism, A Teachable Tale*. Autism Parenting Magazine (Issue 63). www.autismparentingmagazine.com

Maurice, C., Green, G., & Luce, S. C. (1996). *Behavioral Intervention for Young Children with Autism, a Manual for Parents and Professionals.* Pro-ed, Inc.

Merriam Webster Dictionary. merriam-webster.com

One Day University (2010-10-23). *One Day University Presents: Positive Psychology: The Science of Happiness* (Harvard's Most Popular Course) (Kindle Locations 272-273). The Learning Annex. Kindle Edition.

Prizant, B.M., Weatherby, A.M., Rubin, E., Laurent, & A.C., Rydell, P.J. (2006). *The SCERTS Model, a Comprehensive Educational Approach for Children with Autism Spectrum Disorders (Volume II, Program Planning and Intervention).* Paul H. Brookes Publishing Co., Inc.

Reivich, Karen; Shatte, Andrew (2003-10-14). *The Resilience Factor: 7 Keys to Finding Your Inner Strength and Overcoming Life's Hurdles* (Kindle Locations 4386-4387). Potter/TenSpeed/Harmony. Kindle Edition.

Runion, Meryl (2003-12-10). *How to Use Power Phrases to Say What You Mean, Mean What You Say, & Get What You Want* (pp. 122, 171-172). McGraw-Hill. Kindle Edition.

Steve L. (Presenter). (4/23-26/2002). *TEACCH Treatment and Education of Autistic and related Communication Handicapped Children.* Training materials from TEACCH Core Training. Southern California Autism Training Collaborative (SCATC).

Silberman, Mel (2000-05-19). *PeopleSmart: Developing Your Interpersonal Intelligence* (p. 7). Berrett-Koehler Publishers. Kindle Edition.

Thoreau, Henry David (2012-02-28). *The Complete Works of Henry David Thoreau: Canoeing in the Wilderness, Walden, Walking, Civil Disobedience and More* (Kindle Locations 22030-22031). Kindle Edition.

van der Kolk, B. (2014-09-25). *The Body Keeps the Score: Brain, Mind, and Body in the Healing of Trauma* (p. 111). Penguin Publishing Group. Kindle Edition.

Webster's New World College Dictionary (2010) Wiley Publishing, Inc., Cleveland, Ohio. Used by arrangement with John Wiley & Sons, Inc. YourDictionary definition and usage example. Copyright © 2017 by LoveToKnow Corp. Your Dictionary.com

Select MSI Books

Self-Help Books

A Woman's Guide to Self-Nurturing (Romer)

Creative Aging: A Baby Boomer's Guide to Successful Living (Vassiliadis & Romer)

Divorced! Survival Techniques for Singles over Forty (Romer)

How to Get Happy and Stay That Way: Practical Techniques for Putting Joy into Your Life (Romer)

How to Live from Your Heart (Hucknall) (Book of the Year Finalist)

Living Well with Chronic Illness (Charnas)

Overcoming the Odds (C. Leaver)

Publishing for Smarties: Finding a Publisher (Ham)

Recovering from Domestic Violence, Abuse, and Stalking (Romer)

Survival of the Caregiver (Snyder)

The Rose and the Sword: How to Balance Your Feminine and Masculine Energies (Bach & Hucknall)

The Widower's Guide to a New Life (Romer) (Book of the Year Finalist)

Tips and Tools for Living Well with Chronic Illness (Charnas)

Widow: A Survival Guide for the First Year (Romer)

Widow: How to Survive (and Thrive!) in Your 2d, 3d, and 4th Years (Romer)

INSPIRATIONAL AND RELIGIOUS BOOKS

A Believer-in-Waiting's First Encounters with God (Mahlou)

A Guide to Bliss: Transforming Your Life through Mind Expansion (Tubali)

Christmas at the Mission: A Cat's View of Catholic Beliefs and Customs (Sula)

El Poder de lo Transpersonal (Ustman)

Everybody's Little Book of Everyday Prayers (MacGregor)

How to Argue with an Atheist (Brink)

Joshuanism (Tosto)

Living in Blue Sky Mind: Basic Buddhist Teachings for a Happy Life (Diedrichs)

Passing On: How to Prepare Ourselves for the Afterlife (Romer)

Puertas a la Eternidad (Ustman)

Surviving Cancer, Healing People: One Cat's Story (Sula)

Tale of a Mission Cat (Sula)

The Seven Wisdoms of Life: A Journey into the Chakras (Tubali)
(Book of the Year Finalist)

When You're Shoved from the Right, Look to Your Left: Metaphors of Islamic Humanism (O. Imady)

MEMOIRS

57 Steps to Paradise: Finding Love in Midlife and Beyond (Lorenz)

Blest Atheist (Mahlou)

Forget the Goal, the Journey Counts . . . 71 Jobs Later (Stites)

From Deep Within: A Forensic and Clinical Psychologist's Journey (Lewis)

Good Blood: A Journey of Healing (Schaffer)

Healing from Incest: Intimate Conversations with My Therapist (Henderson & Emerton) (Book of the Year Finalist)

It Only Hurts When I Can't Run: One Girl's Story (Parker)

Las Historias de Mi Vida (Ustman)

Of God, Rattlesnakes, and Okra (Easterling)

Road to Damascus (E. Imady)

The Optimistic Food Addict (Fisanick)

Tucker and Me (Harvey)

FOREIGN CULTURE

Syrian Folktales (M. Imady)

The Rise and Fall of Muslim Civil Society (O. Imady)

The Subversive Utopia: Louis Kahn and the Question of National Jewish Style in Jerusalem (Sakr)

Thoughts without a Title (Henderson)

PSYCHOLOGY & PHILOSOPHY

Anger Anonymous: The Big Book on Anger Addiction (Ortman)

Anxiety Anonymous: The Big Book on Anxiety Addiction (Ortman)

PARENTING

365 Teacher Secrets for Parents: Fun Ways to Help Your Child in Elementary School (McKinley & Trombly) [Recommended by US Review of Books; Selected as USA Best Book Finalist]

How to Be a Good Mommy When You're Sick (Graves)

I Am, You Are, My Kid Is... (Leaver)

Lessons of Labor (Aziz)